TEMPLE

without WALLS

Richard Weekley's

Zen Nam

at 76

Zen Nam lives

in an unfurnished compartment
in the author's mind.

ISBN: 978-81-8253-977-8

First Edition: 2022
Rs. 200/-

Cyberwit.net
HIG 45 Kaushambi Kunj, Kalindipuram
Allahabad - 211011 (U.P.) India
http://www.cyberwit.net
Tel: +(91) 9415091004
E-mail: info@cyberwit.net

Printed at Thomson Press India Limited.

Also by Richard J. Weekley

My Small Journey: An Omnibus of Poetry 1981 – 2019

The collected Works including out of print and unavailable books. A rare synchronistic gem of his idiosyncratic voice. It includes Zen Nam's *Still Listening to Ravens* and *Feeling Funny*.

First Insights of a Child (2020)

"If God is everywhere he's in your underwear"

Real utterances, some delightful, some profound typical of the early mind's journey.

Doris Mary Anne Kappelhoff
performed under the name
DORIS DAY

and
Richard John Weekley
sometimes presents under the name
ZEN NAM

It's the simple things in life
that are the most extraordinary.

--Paulo Coelho
The Alchemist

Every word is an unnecessary stain on
SILENCE and NOTHINGNESS.

Samuel Becket

TEMPLE

without

WALLS

Richard Weekley's

Zen Nam

At 76

Then suddenly
Zen Nam was old

He doesn't know how
it happened

He walked with a tilt
and had a tentative
uncertainty
about everything

2-1-22

Zen Nam wonders

why. . .

his shadow
walks
so slow
2/11/22

Zen Nam is not a monk

he even failed
at nothingness
12/17/21

The Universe sent
Zen Nam
a message

in
a cloud code of Japanese
letters

which morphed and faded
in an instant
and *nothing* remained.
3-10-22

Zen Nam's cat

ignores the war news

3-9-22

Zen Nam writes

this poem
[he thinks he'd enlightened –
-- he isn't]

his neighbor
works and bangs
on his used car
and thinks nothing
of enlightenment
[-- he is].
3-2-22

Every time
Zen Nam sends out
a message to the universe
:
it come back
undeliverable

Mailer Daemon
1-7-22

Zen Nam said
no thanks
to a Christian heaven
-
when asked why?
he replied--

"Jesus never jokes"
4-5-22

A stupid student asked
Zen Nam

which was your
best breath?

--

ZN: *they're all good.*
3-21-22

Zen Nam talks to himself
:
his best friend

4-22-22

Zen Nam listens
to the rainbows
crawling his ceiling

and hears every color
clear as a bell

Lizard on a rock
doing
push ups

reminding Zen Nam -
to exercise
9-21-21

Staring contest

Zen Nam
And a gray one inch lizard

9-2-21

640 Million years ago

the last great snows
all over earth
ended

A sunny hot hot morning

The cat lays
in Zen Nam's imperfect
shadow
7-6-21

Mindless

A white butterfly
flits
over the gridlocked cars
-
Who is mindless?
6/12/21

Zen Nam wins
the *humility* competition

for the third year
In a row
-
he even rejected
the golden trophy

A crystal blip
of light
glanced off his eye
-
so it was -
enlightenment passed

4-23-21

Strange day
no wind

Zen Nam heard
perfect stillness
4-29-22

Zen Nam's best part of the day

flushing away yesterday

4-29-22

Drunk with stupidity

Zen Nam
dances like a genius

All day long
it nods
bobs
glistens

top leaf
on a thin branch
4-19-21

Zen Nam
without reaching for stillness

found it

3-30-21

Zen Nam was there

10:13 AM   March 30, 2021

the spring winds arrived

3-30-21

Is it a dove?
or a silhouette of leaves?
riding the tree's big branch

3-30-21

Happy day
spring-like and summer warm

Zen Nam
in flip-flops again
2-5-21

Yesterday
two courting doves
on a tree branch
above him
where Zen Nam lunched

Today
the branch is bare
2-5-21

Zen Nam stokes
each finger

"Don't be sad when I'm gone"
he tells them

1-15-21

Notice –

blue remains
between
the bobbing limbs

1-8-21

Zen Nam notices
it is hard to remember
all the things
he's trying to forget
1-4-21

Listening
to clouds - white
as lumpy dough

Zen Nam
was never happier
4-22-20

Zen Nam's testy reply
to a rude reporter
-
"Don't bother me
I'm growing my nails"

4-22-20

The leaves are
skittering
skittering
skittering

We are leaves
and we are
skittering
skittering
skittering

Zen Nam
was in covid quarantine so long

he tried to divorce himself

pandemic poem

Zen Nam tried
social distancing

But no matter how hard he
tried

He couldn't stay away
from himself

Zen Nam asked himself

"What in the hell do you think you're doing?"

Smart as a whip
he refused answer
and took the Fifth Amendment

Zen Nam blessed

he sees
the miraculous scoot
of a tiny lizard

and simultaneously
smells Jasmine in bloom

5-4-20

The unexpected

raven door mat
arrived in a box

Zen Nam
wiped his feet
on the beak
2-12-18

Do trees dream?

Zen Nam dissatisfied

with one mirror

so tries another

Turn me on
She said

Zen Nam pressed
the button

on her oxygen machine
11-18-19

Zen Nam sustains injury

patting himself on the back

8-1-19

She asked me this morning “if she was already dead”

wrote Zen Nam’s friend
about his wife

she can barely walk
or breathe
she doesn’t eat

she got up last night
and started getting dressed
because she thought
she had to go somewhere.

7-28-19

Zen Nam forgets humility

"my book is bigger than yours"

7-25-19

Zen Nam sinks to a new depth

uses a leaf blower
to clean the hut

7-10-19

Zen Nam discovers

27 feathers on the floor

the cat ignored
his canned tuna that night

7-25-19

No one can replace Danny

he had a heart attack
day before yesterday

he was the only one at a party
who could dance
with his drink
balanced on his head

5-2-22

You cannot know stillness unless you first know the wind

Under the Bedspread

cat hides

-

fourth of July fireworks.

7-4-19

Moments

the more we squeeze

the faster they die

Rata-tat-tat
Rata-tat-tat
Rata-tat-tat

Zen Nam awakens

jackhammering at the corner

Zen Nam - strange joke

God: "How was I"

Mary: "O God you were good"

From the book: *All You Wanted to Know about Immaculate Conception But Were Afraid to Ask*

At noon an old, tall, skinny man
walked slowly by Zen Nam's hut

talking loudly to himself (as usual)

6-4-13

Zen Nam read about
the last monk in the monastery
who polished his bones
and
broke all the rules
he never made

2-3-19

**Zen Nam's gets
counseling
*
at night
tells his problems

to the wag
and slow un-curlings
of the cat's long black tail.**

5-9-22

Zen Nam walks
out of a restaurant
loaded with take home boxes

not realizing
he'd gathered up the unpaid
check as well.
1-3-19

Perfect moment

NO
messages, calls or emails

no replies needed
ahhhh
11-25-18

Zen Nam determined

to fire his sloppy,
lazy gardener

then realized
he'd be out of his only job
11-19-18

Not Useless

Dead barren tree limbs
twisting catawampus high
into hazy blue

four happy doves on a limb
in morning sun
preen and coo

10-25-18

When flimsy tendrils stir

Zen Nam knows

there is a breeze

10-24-18

**Like reading tea leaves
Zen Nam ponders**

**a raven's white defecation
on his patio chair**

10-13-18

Like you

Zen Nam wonders - - what's next?

5-9-22

Always something

Once it was pimples

now it's age spots

Forever expanding faster and faster

TEMPLE WITHOUT WALLS

5-15-22

www.ingramcontent.com/pod-product-compliance
Lightning Source LLC
Chambersburg PA
CBHW022202160726
48282CB00024B/299
9788182539778